ONE ARM

BY
MOISÉS KAUFMAN

BASED ON THE SHORT STORY
AND SCREENPLAY BY
TENNESSEE WILLIAMS

★

DRAMATISTS
PLAY SERVICE
INC.

SPECIAL NOTE

Anyone receiving permission to produce ONE ARM is required to give credit to the Author as sole and exclusive Author of the Play, and to Tennessee Williams as sole author of the underlying work, on the title page of all programs distributed in connection with performances of the Play and in all instances in which the title of the Play appears for purposes of advertising, publicizing or otherwise exploiting the Play and/or a production thereof. The name of the Author and the name of Tennessee Williams must appear on a separate line in which no other name appears, immediately beneath the title and in size of type equal to 50% of the size of the largest, most prominent letter used for the title of the Play. The name of Tennessee Williams shall appear in the same size of type and prominence as that of the Author. No person, firm or entity may receive credit larger or more prominent than that accorded the Author. The billing must appear as follows:

ONE ARM
by Moisés Kaufman
based on the short story and screenplay
by Tennessee Williams

The following acknowledgment must appear on the title page in all programs distributed in connection with performances of the Play, and in all advertising and publicity in which full production credits appear. The following credit shall be clear and prominent, in size of type not less than 25% of the size of the Author's billing:

Produced in New York City
by The New Group (Scott Elliot, Artistic Director)
and Tectonic Theater Project (Moisés Kaufman, Artistic Director)
by arrangement with the University of the South, Sewanee, Tennessee.

SPECIAL NOTE ON SONGS AND RECORDINGS

For performances of copyrighted songs, arrangements or recordings mentioned in this Play, the permission of the copyright owner(s) must be obtained. Other songs, arrangements or recordings may be substituted provided permission from the copyright owner(s) of such songs, arrangements or recordings is obtained; or songs, arrangements or recordings in the public domain may be substituted.

ADAPTOR'S NOTE

In 1942 Tennessee Williams wrote a short story entitled "One Arm." This story must have stayed with him, because twenty-five years later, in 1967, he wrote a screenplay based on it. Although he tried for the rest of his life to get this movie made, he never succeeded.

When I first read the screenplay, I was struck by its frankness and emotional rawness. In it Williams portrays a world he knew intimately with remarkable honesty and candor. And it felt revelatory to me, not only about Williams himself, but about an often overlooked narrative thread in American history.

This adaptation is not — nor does it pretend to be — a realistic play. I'm interested in exploring theatrical forms (as was Williams himself), and in that context this adaptation uses the stage to allow the audience to imagine the movie that was never made. In this experiment, the actors use the tag lines from the screenplay, the voiceover narration, and the text Williams wrote as stage directions to allow the audience to imagine the film. By doing this, we've created a sort of "theatrical screenplay."

Working with dramaturgs Jimmy Maize and David Schultz, we located several drafts of the screenplay in libraries and private collections at Harvard University, Columbia University and the New York Public Library. Each version led us to a deeper understanding of the story, characters and themes Williams was exploring.

In this adaptation I've used texts from these different drafts, as well as sections of the short story.

A short design note: In production, we found that having the stage loosely suggest a prison (without realistically depicting one) allowed us the possibility to easily create all the other locations called for in the text.

ONE ARM received its world premiere in Chicago, Illinois, presented by About Face Theatre and Tectonic Theater Project, at the Steppenwolf Theatre on December 2, 2004. It was directed by Moisés Kaufman; the set design was by Derek McLane; the costume design was by Janice Pytel; the lighting design was by Mike Baldassari; and the sound design and music were by Andre Pluess. The cast was as follows:

Marilyn Bielby, Josh Bywater, Jason Denuszek, Steve Key, Sandra Marquez, John McAdams, David Parkes, Reynaldo Rosales, Kelli Simpkins, Michael Stahl-David, Joe Van Slyke, Eltony Williams and Shané Williams.

ONE ARM was subsequently presented by The New Group (Scott Elliott, Artistic Director; Geoff Rich, Executive Director) and Tectonic Theater Project (Moisés Kaufman, Artistic Director; Greg Reiner, Executive Director; Tiffany Redmon, General Manager) at the Acorn Theater in New York City, opening on May 19, 2011. It was directed by Moisés Kaufman; the dramaturgs were Jimmy Maize and David G. Schultz; the set design was by Derek McLane; the costume design was by Clint Ramos; the lighting design was by David Lander; the music and sound design were by Shane Rettig; the production stage manager was Valerie A. Peterson; and the associate director was Jimmy Maize. The cast was as follows:

NARRATOR / SEAN / ENSEMBLE . . . . Noah Bean
WILLY / SAILOR / ENSEMBLE . . . . K C Comeaux
OLLIE OLSEN . . . . Claybourne Elder
LESTER / CHAPLAIN / ENSEMBLE . . . . Steven Hauck
DIVINITY STUDENT / SAILOR / MIDDLE-AGED
HOMOSEXUAL / ENSEMBLE . . . . Todd Lawson
PRISON GUARD / YACHTSMAN /
ENSEMBLE . . . . Christopher McCann
CHERRY / MAN IN THE PARK / MIDDLE-AGED
HOMOSEXUAL / MRS. WIRE / THE WARDEN /
ENSEMBLE . . . . Greg Pierotti
LILA / GIRL IN THE FRENCH QUARTER /
NURSE / ENSEMBLE . . . . Larisa Polonsky

CHARACTERS

OLLIE

NARRATOR/SEAN

SAM a hot tamale vendor

WILLY, another male hustler

A MIDDLE-AGED HOMOSEXUAL MAN

SAILORS

A STRIPPER

THE YOUNG MAN IN THE PARK

BARTENDER

THE YACHTSMAN

THE GIRL ON THE YACHT

ANOTHER MIDDLE-AGED HOMOSEXUAL MAN

LESTER, a middle-aged homosexual

A GIRL IN THE FRENCH QUARTER

CHERRY, an old queen

THE PRISON GUARD

THE PRISON CHAPLAIN

THE DIVINITY STUDENT

SEVERAL VOICES

MRS. WIRE, a landlady

THE WARDEN

ONE ARM

The company of actors enters the stage. The Narrator holds up a copy of the screenplay and says:

NARRATOR/SEAN. *One Arm,* an unproduced screenplay by Tennessee Williams. *(He reads.)* Fade in. Close up on Ollie. *(Ollie steps center stage.)* A voiceover narration begins. *(The Narrator sits down as his table and reads from the screenplay. While he reads, the other actors surround Ollie and buckle a leather strap around his right arm to prevent its mobility.)* The young man, so young you could call him a boy, is an actor, of course, and in the part that he's going to perform he's supposed to have only one arm. He's supposed to have only one arm except in a few short scenes that will show how the arm was lost. In the film you'll notice that one of his arms is never lifted, never used. Think of it as an arm that doesn't exist. Dissolve to interior. Prison. Day. Ollie is alone. The cell is the "birdcage," reserved for the soon to be executed — no windows. *(Ollie is alone in his prison cell.)*

GUARD. Letters for you. Quite a few.

OLLIE. I been all around the country and made lots of friendly contacts here and there.

GUARD. Want to keep 'em or have 'em burned?

OLLIE. I want to keep them. They're mine.

GUARD. Very interesting.

OLLIE. What?

GUARD. No return addresses.

OLLIE. So?

GUARD. And such fine paper. Mmmm. They smell good.

OLLIE. Give me my letters. *(The guard gives them to Ollie. He opens and reads a letter.)*

CORRESPONDENT 1. "Dear Ollie, I saw your photograph in a newspaper and of course I recognized you at once. I can't believe what

they are saying about you. It's like a bad dream. The Ollie they are describing is not the person I know. I am certain there must be some sort of mistake. Are they planning an appeal? Is there anything I can do to help?" *(Ollie puts down the letter and opens another, reading.)*
CORRESPONDENT 2. "Dear Ollie, I can't believe this is happening to you. I've been following your story every day. Can what they are saying be true? It can't be. Thinking back on New Orleans, all I remember is what a friendly sort of fellow you were and what a good experience knowing you was. Is there any chance left of an appeal?" *(Ollie crumples up the letters and throws them into the trash.)*

Transition into Canal Street.

COMPANY MEMBER. Dissolve to exterior. New Orleans. Canal Street. Day.
OLLIE. *(Calling to someone in the street.)* Hey, Sam! *(A hot tamale vendor, Sam, enters and rolls his steaming cart to the curb where Ollie stands.)* Gimme half-a-dozen tamales. Need something hot in my belly. Whoever said you don't freeze y'r balls off in this town never hit it in winter.
SAM. Whyn't you wear something' warmer?
WILLY. *(Entering.)* Ollie's gotta show his merchandise.
OLLIE. Unpeel these fo' me, Willy.
WILLY. *(Unpeeling a tamale.)* You know, I seen a guy with no arms in a sideshow that could cut and butter a piece of toast with his toes.
OLLIE. I ain't in no sideshow. *(Willy is eating the tamale himself.)* What the fuck you — ?
WILLY. Took a percentage for labor. *(He has unpeeled the second tamale; he tries to stick it in Ollie's mouth for him.)*
OLLIE. *(Abruptly savage.)* Quit clowning! *(He seizes the tamale from Willy and wolfs it down. He grimaces.)* This stuff's rat meat an' pepper but it warms your stomach. You can have the rest. *(We hear a sea gull's thin, anxious cry.)* Somebody tole me that if you stand in one place long enough near the sea or the Gulf — *(He grins slowly.)* a sea gull will fly over and shit a pot of gold on you. *(He laughs harshly.)* Is that a fact or a fiction? *(Willy laughs bleakly.)* You scored yet today?

WILLY. *(Shaking his head.)* This is a bitch of a day.

OLLIE. Still too early for action. Work that other corner and tell your sister Kewpie to work on Bourbon, up, down, and sideways. She needs t' walk some of that baby fat off her ass an' git an ID card so she can operate in gay bars.

WILLY. He's too young, they don't let her into gay bars.

OLLIE. If she could grow a little mustache or beard she'd pass for seventeen maybe.

WILLY. Kewpie? She can't even shave yet.

OLLIE. She might be a morphodite but she could attract older johns that dig chicken. She needs a faked ID card to get her in places like Mona's, and some new clean threads.

WILLY. They kicked us out of Mona's two days ago.

OLLIE. That's 'cause you oughta separate when you're workin', you camp an' giggle together, come on like a pair of sisters.

WILLY. Voice of authority?

OLLIE. Voice of three years' experience, enough t' know.

WILLY. That Kewpie, shit. *(He grins.)* Father Rogers from Saint Jude just now talked a man out of jumpin' off a tenth-floor window ledge at the Pere Marquette building. The Father held up a cross an' shouted through a megaphone, "Christ loves you. Don't jump." An' that Kewpie, he hollers back, "Christ don't know you! Jump!" — Got kicked in the ass by a cop.

OLLIE. Guys that jump out windows mess up streets. *(Willy grins widely at this.)* You oughta see a dentist. That missing tooth makes you look morbid.

WILLY. You got to pay for a tooth that ain't your own … I see an old john I blown for five bucks back of the Pirate's. *(He crosses quickly out.)*

OLLIE. *(Directly out.)* That's the name of the game. That's the goddamn name of the game. *(Middle-aged man enters.)*

NARRATOR/SEAN. A middle-aged man has stopped on the walk a few yards from Ollie and is looking at the contents of a shop window. Ollie appears not to see him, you'd think Ollie was looking at a sea gull in the sky. The middle-aged man stops now closer to Ollie and looks in another shop window with blinded eyes. Maybe the boy is employed by the police. He is waiting for Ollie to give him a sign of interest. Now Ollie gives him the sign the cautious john was waiting for. He jingles the keys and coins in his pocket.

MIDDLE-AGED MAN. Aren't you afraid of catching cold, young fellow?
OLLIE. No, sir. I never catch cold.
MIDDLE-AGED MAN. But you feel cold, don't you?
OLLIE. Yes, I feel cold. I'm not unconscious.
MIDDLE-AGED MAN. I hope I'm not being too personal, but I might add you've got a wonderful build.
OLLIE. Thanks.
MIDDLE-AGED MAN. Do you, uh, work out in a gym, or …
OLLIE. No, sir. *(Then, he continues with a quiet, sad pride.)* — I used to be light heavyweight champion of the Pacific Fleet.
MIDDLE-AGED MAN. Before you —
OLLIE. Yes. Before I lost one arm.
MIDDLE-AGED MAN. You ought to go in somewhere and get warmed up.
OLLIE. Such as where, for instance?
MIDDLE-AGED MAN. I have a nice apartment, and a good supply of liquor.
OLLIE. Which way?
MIDDLE-AGED MAN. A few blocks, in the Quarter. We'll take a cab. *(Pause.)* So, you want to come with me?
OLLIE. Let's walk and you give me the cab fare.
COMPANY MEMBER. Dissolve to interior. Middle-aged man's apartment. *(The man caresses Ollie's chest. He holds Ollie's hand, kisses it, then places it on his chest. Ollie pulls away from the man.)*

Transition into jail.

The guard enters.

GUARD. More letters for ya.
OLLIE. What'd you say to me?
GUARD. More letters for you. Sure are getting popular.
OLLIE. What's'a'matter? You jealous?
GUARD. What?
OLLIE. I seen you sittin' up there all day. Nobody write to you? *(Pause.)*

GUARD. Hmm, I don't see no letter from the governor yet. I guess that means no pardon for you. You know what they say: "no news is bad news." *(The Guard throws them down on the floor and leaves.)*
OLLIE. Bastard!

Transition to a boxing ring.

The bell rings. We hear the crowd.

ANNOUNCER. And here we are in the fifth round in the San Diego Forum. It's been quite a fight so far — the challenger Ollie Olsen struggling valiantly against reigning champion Myers. Olsen is tired and bleeding over his right eye. I don't know how much more of this he can take … *(Bell rings.)* Myers comes right to the center of the ring. Olsen is cautiously circling him. Olsen misses with his left. Myers lands a hard right to the body. Olsen staggers back. Back in the center of the ring. Olsen lands a short jab. And another. The tide seems to be shifting here for Olsen. Olsen is right on him. Attacking his body. A flurry of blows to the ribs. Myers pushes Olsen away. Desperately defending himself. A wild swing by Myers. Olsen dodges. Ollie Olsen hits Meyers with a blinding right hook! That's why he's known as "lightning in leather." Olsen's swift right hand has knocked Myers down. He doesn't seem to be getting up. Time is running out … 7, 8, 9, 10. He is down for the count! What an unbelievable comeback for Ollie Olsen! The winner and new light heavyweight champion of the Pacific Fleet, Ollie "Lightning in Leather"! Folks, this is one for the record books — in all my years I have never seen anything like it! Ollie Olsen has made history here tonight! That's right — he has made boxing history here tonight!

Transition to Ollie driving a car with two sailors.

FIRST SAILOR. Ladies and gentleman introducing the new light heavyweight champion of the Pacific Fleet. Ollie-Lightning-In-Leather-Olsen. Otherwise known as "Arkansas!"
SECOND SAILOR. "Arkansas!" *(They celebrate.)* Today, he's the champion of the Pacific Fleet. Tomorrow — the entire Navy!
FIRST SAILOR. The entire country!
SECOND SAILOR. The entire world!
OLLIE. Hey, Shelley, you drive terrible. You almost hit that old man.
FIRST SAILOR. Oh, come on, it wasn't even close
OLLIE. Wasn't even close? Look at 'em, he's lying on the ground.
FIRST SAILOR. He's fine. *(The car stops. Engine off.)* Come on, let's go inside. *(They exit the car.)*
OLLIE. No it's not fine. You shouldn't be driving like that.
FIRST SAILOR. It's a nice night to celebrate.
OLLIE. Celebrate, celebrate, listen I'm gonna go in here with you boys, but when we hit the road again I'm driving. You hear me?

Transition into a strip club. A stripper is performing. The boys celebrate as the stripper dances with Ollie.

NARRATOR/SEAN. His experience was limited. He came from the cotton fields of Arkansas, where he had known only hard work in the sun and such emotional adventures as farm boys have on Saturday nights and Sunday afternoons. So he had only a very tentative knowledge of girls. *(The boys are leaving the strip club and getting into the car.)*
FIRST SAILOR. Come on Romeo. Some woman that was! Glory Blaze! Older'n my mother. A pig.
OLLIE. Good enough for me.
FIRST SAILOR. Open all night!
OLLIE. All night!
FIRST SAILOR. Imagine those women at the end of all night. *(First sailor takes out his keys.)*
OLLIE. Shelley, didn't you hear me say I drive if you drink?
FIRST SAILOR. Shit, come off it, git in.
OLLIE. I'll drive this heap or go back to the base in a cab. Seriously, you guys don't value your lives, I value mine. Gimme the keys, Shelley! *(They laugh at him. He attempts to hail a cab.)*

FIRST SAILOR. Okay, Eagle Scout, catch a cab!

OLLIE. All right, fine. *(Ollie steps away and starts shouting.)* Cab, cab! Hey cab! Come on! *(Sound of cars zooming by.)*

FIRST SAILOR. Ollie thinks he's ape-shit t'night, let him go. Where's your cab, Ollie? *(Ollie, reluctantly, returns to the car, and gets inside.)*

OLLIE. Alright, fine.

FIRST SAILOR. Ah, he's back!

COMPANY MEMBER. Dissolve to exterior. Highway. Night.

OLLIE. Shelley, slow down.

FIRST SAILOR. It's called "having fun," Arkansas..

NARRATOR/SEAN. The car, driven at high speed, approaches an underpass.

OLLIE. Shelley, come on. Slow down! *(We hear a car crash.)*

NARRATOR/SEAN. The two sailors in the car have been killed outright. Ollie got off the lightest with just the loss of an arm. Ollie was admitted to the hospital, Hotel Dieu, "God's Hospital" in French — a language Ollie doesn't know. *(A nurse appears.)*

NURSE. Ollie, you're being too bitter about that accident, that loss. You're not being grown-up about it. Of course boxing isn't life for you, now. You've got to face that loss. Everyone here is adjusting to losses, some of them worse than yours. Ollie, We know the strain you're under, how hard it is to accept the loss of an arm, but some-day you'll accept it so much you'll ignore it. If you have trouble with balance, you can use a wheelchair or a crutch for a while.

OLLIE. When I leave here, it ain't gonna be in a wheelchair or on a crutch. I'm gonna walk out balanced on my own two feet, that's how.

NARRATOR/SEAN. After he left the hospital, he looked for employment — I mean legitimate jobs, you know. Nobody wants to hire a man with one arm. He'd hit the city with money, but money moves, and the way it moves in Ollie's case is away. After a week he couldn't afford to eat anywhere better than "The Parkway."

COMPANY MEMBER. Dissolve to exterior. New Orleans. Night. The camera pans around a park bench to reveal Ollie.

YOUNG MAN. I haven't seen you in the park before.

OLLIE. That might be because I ain't been in it before.

YOUNG MAN. Mind if I sit down?

OLLIE. You're already sittin'. *(Ollie devours the last bit of the drip-*

ping hot dog and licks the fingers of his hand.)
YOUNG MAN. Handkerchief?
OLLIE. No, thanks. *(The young man applies the handkerchief to his chin. Ollie pushes it away.)* What are you doing?
YOUNG MAN. You spilt some of the chili on your chin, which, incidentally, honey, needs shaving. A boy with your looks shouldn't neglect them, you know. I'll tell you something else. You ought to be having sirloin steak for dinner instead of a greasy hot dog.
OLLIE. By the end of the week, I won't be able to afford even this.
YOUNG MAN. I have a feeling that you don't know the score. Honey, I don't think you're even aware that four johns in this park are watching you like bird dogs watching a game bird. That one, look, that one, that one and that one.
OLLIE. Why?
YOUNG MAN. Your innocence would be incredible in anyone but you. Those johns are hungry, they're ravenous for you. Let's break their hearts by walking around the fountain together, huh?
OLLIE. G'night.
YOUNG MAN. Not that direction. The other. I want to treat you to a thick malt, and give you a quick education in the mysteries of the park. Come on. It won't take long. *(The young man is seen undressing and dressing Ollie — a transformation of sorts into a hustler.)*
NARRATOR/SEAN. The young man wised Ollie up to his commodity value and how to cash in on it. Within a month the one-armed youth was fully inured to the practices and the culture of the underworld that seethed around the bars of the Vieux Carre and benchlined walks of the park, and foreign as it was, the shock that it gave him was slight. The loss of the arm had apparently dulled his senses. With it had gone his wholesome propriety. Now he could feel no shame that green soap and water did not remove well enough to satisfy him.

Transition — back to the street corner in opening scene.

MIDDLE-AGED MAN #2. Aren't you afraid of catching cold, young fellow?
OLLIE. No, sir. I never catch cold.

MIDDLE-AGED MAN #2. But you feel cold, don't you?
OLLIE. Yes, I feel cold. I'm not unconscious.
MIDDLE-AGED MAN #2. And I might add, you've got a wonderful build.
OLLIE. *(With no perceptible reaction.)* Thanks.
MIDDLE-AGED MAN #2. Do you, uh, work out in a gym, or …
OLLIE. No, sir. *(Then, he continues with a quiet, sad pride.)* — I used to be light heavyweight champion of the Pacific Fleet.
MIDDLE-AGED MAN #2. Before you —
OLLIE. Yes. Before I lost one arm.
MIDDLE-AGED MAN #2. You ought to go in somewhere and get warmed up.
OLLIE. Such as where, for instance?
MIDDLE-AGED MAN #2. I have a nice apartment, and a good supply of liquor.
OLLIE. Which way?
MIDDLE-AGED MAN #2. A few blocks, in the Quarter. We'll take a cab. You gonna come with me?
OLLIE. Let's walk and you give me the cab fare.

Transition.

The middle-aged man backs away from Ollie, as we transition into the prison. The guard enters sifting through Ollie's letters.

GUARD. Ollie Olsen, Ollie Olsen — Look at all these letters. Even the postman wonders how you got so popular. Look here: General Delivery Memphis, General Delivery Kansas City, General Delivery New Orleans.
MIDDLE-AGED MAN #2. Dear Ollie, I'm writing you this letter because I saw your picture in the paper this morning.
GUARD. General Delivery: Cincinnati.
MIDDLE-AGED MAN #2. I remember the time we spent together in New Orleans, but I never thought I'd see you again.
GUARD. General Delivery: Savannah.
MIDDLE-AGED MAN #2. But your picture in my local news-

paper brought you back to me.

GUARD. General Delivery: Charlotte.

MIDDLE-AGED MAN #2. I can't believe you're guilty of what you're accused of — I truly hope that justice will be done in the end.

GUARD. Oh my, look at you! — Mr. General Delivery!

NARRATOR/SEAN. There were so many of them, the queer, the not-so-young-anymore with their loneliness a terrible cry in their throats. We can't play back all their voices or deal out all their photos like a gypsy's deck of filthy, dog-eared cards, telling always almost the same fortune both to them and the boy. He must have known, he must have realized with God knows how much dread — that he'd have to surrender a bit, and then a bit more, and more and more and more … And yet there was this one time when —

Transition to The French Quarter. Ollie is with a girl, just outside her building. It has just stopped raining. The girl juggles a wet umbrella as she fumbles for her keys; Ollie's thin clothes are soaked.

GIRL. *(Unlocking the gate.)* There, now! The key was the last thing I could locate in my bag! Watch your step on these bricks, they're the original bricks of the patio — which is called the slave quarters, you know.

OLLIE. Slaves used to live back here?

GIRL. Yes there were slaves in all these old houses … in the *Vieux Carre,* which is also called the French Quarter, you know.

OLLIE. Yeah, I know about that. It's quiet here, not a sound.

GIRL. Now I have to locate another key, and I hope I'll be luckier this time.

OLLIE. Want me to do it for you since you've got shaky fingers?

GIRL. Found! Found!

OLLIE. Good.

GIRL. When I was looking for a little apartment in the Quarter, there were two vacancies here. One was very inexpensive in spite

of having much better facilities, even a rotisserie in it for cooking at home, but the other apartment we'll soon be in — I really couldn't afford it — I chose it for a particular reason you'll see in just a moment. *(She gets the door open.)*
GIRL. There, now! Who enters first?
OLLIE. You better, I don't know the place.
GIRL. You go in first. I want to see if you see the particular reason I took it.
OLLIE. Okay, I'll go in first. *(They go inside and Ollie begins to strike a match.)*
GIRL. No, no, no, no match!
OLLIE. I think you took it because of the skylight.
GIRL. That's the reason, exactly. — Shall I turn on a lamp or is the skylight enough?
OLLIE. Enough for me.
GIRL. Enough for me, too. There aren't any chairs in the room, not a single chair, so you have to choose between the floor and the bed under the skylight. But the first thing I want you to do, if you'll oblige me, is get out of those wet things and rub yourself dry with a towel. Here's the towel. Do you want to undress in the room or in the bathroom? No, no, do it in here, and then, after that lie down on the bed under the skylight and look up at those low clouds running over like a parade of enormous roses. They're lighted by the neon signs downtown. But I'd rather think that they had the light from inside them. Get out of your wet things and I'll rub you dry with the towel.
OLLIE. I can do it myself.
GIRL. I know you could, but don't deprive me of — the enjoyment, please.
OLLIE. What?
GIRL. The enjoyment, please. I'm a trained nurse so you mustn't feel any embarrassment with me.
OLLIE. I don't feel any. There aren't many things I feel. As a trained nurse, could you explain that to me?
GIRL. You just lie down under the skylight and I'll try to explain it to you. I think it has something to do with — before you lost one arm did you feel things more? *(Ollie speaks an indistinct syllable.)* Did you say yes or no?
OLLIE. Yes. Naturally.
GIRL. How recently did you lose it?
OLLIE. A few years ago. I was an athlete then.

GIRL. And since that time you've felt —

OLLIE. Less and less and less all the time.

GIRL. You feel less because you feel that you're mutilated. Do you mind if I ask you how you lost your arm?

OLLIE. In a car crash. Are you bothered by it?

GIRL. Of course not. What you should feel is the truth. The loss of one arm makes you look like a — piece of antique sculpture.

OLLIE. Is that good?

GIRL. It makes you — more attractive.

OLLIE. Some people are maybe attracted by mutilation but the person that has the mutilation, he isn't attracted by it, and that's for sure. Sometimes it — in my own case, it fouled up my life. I live a fouled-up life and I'm disgusted by it.

GIRL. — What do you do?

OLLIE. — I — live.

GIRL. I mean what for a living. *(Pause.)*

OLLIE. That corner where we met, I stand on that corner from ten in the morning till midnight.

GIRL. Doing what?

OLLIE. All right. Waiting to be picked up. *(Pause.)* Well?

GIRL. You have a place to stay — somewhere to go?

OLLIE. Yes. I have a room.

GIRL. It's three A.M. and I go on duty at the hospital at seven A.M. I ought to sleep now instead of shacking up with a male prostitute.

OLLIE. You mean you want me to go.

GIRL. I'm afraid that's just exactly what I mean.

OLLIE. — I'll go. I'll go right away. I'll go right away!

Transition. The Girl's room is back to being the prison.

GUARD. You've been screaming all night, and If you don't stop we're gonna turn the fire hose on you! Is that what you want?! You're in the state penitentiary, and you're gonna learn how we do things here!

COMPANY MEMBER. Dissolve to exterior. Rooming house. Night.

OLLIE. I come to say goodbye.

SEAN. Shhh. *(We hear the landlady mutter in her sleep.)*
WIRE. Can't run a clean house in the Quarter. Bunch a crackpots and deadbeats — *(She snores.)* degenerates…
SEAN. That witch of a landlady, she sleeps on a cot in the hall so no one can come or go without her knowing it.
OLLIE. Sorry Sean, I wouldn't have come this late if I wasn't leavin' town so early.
SEAN. You're leaving New Orleans?
OLLIE. Yep. At seven A.M. I made my bus fare t'night.
SEAN. — I'll —
OLLIE. Huh?
SEAN. Miss you, Ollie. *(They smile at each other sadly and shyly.)* Well, sit down. I'm sorry I've got no liquor left.
OLLIE. I don't need no drink. — were you writing?
SEAN. I was trying to write with a pencil. I think one leg of this goddamn table is shorter than the others, but I couldn't discover which leg it was, and — You know, when I work with my typewriter, it makes so much racket that I don't notice the creaking of the table. I was relieved when you interrupted the — *(Ollie has snatched the matchbook from under one leg of the table and inserts it beneath another.)*
OLLIE. There now. — Where's your typewriter?
SEAN. — On vacation.
OLLIE. You mean in a Rampart Street hock shop. How much did you get for it? Ten bucks?
SEAN. Five. He said it had deteriorated in value. From use and abuse.
OLLIE. Fuggin' sharks. *(He peels off a ten spot and puts it on the table.)* Here! Write up my life story.
SEAN. You can't write up a life story till the subject is dead.
OLLIE. I been dead a few years.
SEAN. You can't afford to —
OLLIE. If I couldn't afford to, I wouldn't. I — made fifty bucks t'night from a single john. Take it. *(Ollie hands him the money.)*
SEAN. Thank you.
OLLIE. Jesus, I never known a morphodite with a perversion like he had.
SEAN. Oh?
OLLIE. He ast me to — *(Pause.)*
SEAN. What did he ask you to do?
OLLIE. — To — *(In the bar, half a block away, a piano is playing*

blues.) Human perversions. There's no limit to them. This lunatic I went with t'night, he wasn't unusual lookin'. But on the way to his pad, he kept bringin' up the subject of — "Do you feel like takin' a pee?" Well, I did. I said — "Wait a minute for me outside the next bar we pass." "No, no. Hold it till we're home."

SEAN. Oh. He wanted what is called a golden shower.

OLLIE. I'd never run into a thing like that before. He got onto his knees with his arms around mine and — I kicked his mouth to break away from him.

SEAN. I understand.

WIRE'S VOICE. Somebody's sneaked somebody up there.

SEAN. Shitty landlord.

OLLIE. After the crash, they put me in this hospital, Hotel Dieu. That means God's Hotel.

SEAN. I didn't know he was in the hotel business.

OLLIE. All landlords are the same ...

WIRE'S VOICE. Everybody will stick to house regulations or get the hell out! I'll open the doors and howl for the police if this goes on!

OLLIE. Lately, I've thought of goin' north. This thing that happened t'night convinced me it's time to.

SEAN. Ollie, stay. There are plenty of jobs here now —

OLLIE. Don't you think I've tried? Nobody wants to hire a man with one arm. *(Pause.)* I'm moving to New York, Sean. Do you know how much money people can make doin' my line of work up there? I'll do it for a year, tops — make some real money — and then quit this racket for good. I've valuated your friendship because it was always decent. Good luck, Sean. Write good an' take care. Take care. *(He throws money at the bed and begins to leave.)*

SEAN. Take care.

OLLIE. Take care. *(He leaves.)*

NARRATOR/SEAN. He collected his things and disappeared from the city. He tried to keep to less conspicuous channels losing himself in the swarm of his fugitive kind wherever a town was large enough for such traffic to pass without too much attention. He moved among figures as tenuous as shadows working his way to New York. The city didn't surprise him. In fact nothing did that happened. He learned the ropes at once. Gradually he began to notice where the better hustlers make out in that imperial city. He went to work for Cherry, an old queen who ran a high-priced call house for boys. He'd check in about eight o'clock and sit around playing poker, exchanging jokes and telling stories of his experiences. *(The phone rings.)* The phone would ring every couple of minutes, and Cherry would say:

CHERRY. Hey it's Cherry. *(Beat.)* Yeah. Yeah. I've got just the right person for you. *(Beat.)* Whenever you want. In an hour? *(Beat.)* Yes, he'll be there. Bye. *(He hangs up the phone.)* Ollie, this john wants you. This john is good for whatever you're good enough for. Pretend you don't notice the yellow toupee on his head. Tell him you just come in town from … Idaho or somewhere. I think you're right for him, Ollie. Here's the address. It's the penthouse apartment. His name is Lester Dubinski. He likes to talk, you know, to come on intellectual. Get the picture, Ollie?
OLLIE. Hell, I painted the picture!

Music — Transition into Lester's apartment. Dietrich, perhaps. *

OLLIE. I been in town just three days, Les.
LESTER. But you've already met Cherry.
OLLIE. Yes, accidentally, yes. I was comin' out of the library.
LESTER. With a book?
OLLIE. Yeah, with a book.
LESTER. What was the title of it?
OLLIE. — The name of the book?
LESTER. Yes, its title. I'm interested in your taste in reading matter.
OLLIE. — It was — *(Pause.)*
LESTER. — You've forgotten the title of the book? *(He laughs.)*
OLLIE. I ain't forgotten. It was named *The Care and Preservation of Male Hair.*
LESTER. *(He laughs uncomfortably.)* Why would that subject interest a man with such crowning glory as yours?
OLLIE. I thought sometime in the future my hair might start to go on me.
LESTER. — Oh.

* See Special Note on Songs and Recordings on copyright page.

OLLIE. Yes …

LESTER. Would you like a little more brandy?

OLLIE. My mother, back on the farm in Idaho, the last thing she said to me was, "Son, watch out for liquor." — I guess she meant I should keep an eye on it so it wouldn't escape me.

LESTER. Courvoisier again, or Rémy Martin?

OLLIE. Two jiggers of Five-Star Hennessy in that fishbowl, please.

LESTER. I'm literally astounded that an Idaho farm boy would know the names of brandy.

OLLIE. Well, the Idaho farm was a swinging place. My father played a harpsichord and mother doubled in brass.

LESTER. What did you play?

OLLIE. I had those gourds that you rattle.

LESTER. *(Handing the brandy to Ollie.)* Voici! — Idaho farmboy.

OLLIE. Thanks. You know I really admire your terrace.

LESTER. It is wonderful, isn't it?

OLLIE. Mm.

LESTER. Central Park.

OLLIE. How many floors up?

LESTER. Thirty-seven up and the same number down. *(Beat.)* — Do you have impulses of self-destruction?

OLLIE. — Why'd you ask me that?

LESTER. Because, I have them. I suppose that's why. Listen. *(They listen to the music.)* The inimitable [Dietrich], imperishable as the sky. Let's go back in. Even in summer, I shiver on this terrace. *(They return to the living room. As Ollie passes, Lester slides a hand down his back. The hand stops at Ollie's buttocks.)* Mmm. Classic callipygian. Did they teach you what that means in Idaho? It means narrow hips with high, prominent buttocks.

OLLIE. Les, you're out of bounds. Know what that means, Les?

LESTER. *(Reluctantly dropping his hand.)* Yes. — Sorry. — What a pity!

OLLIE. How much do you pay a month for this apartment?

LESTER. Nothing at all, this apartment is a co-op. *(The record ends.)*

OLLIE. It's a — what did you say it was?

LESTER. Cooperative apartment.

OLLIE. Cooperating with what?

LESTER. *(He laughs at this.)* Shall we have some more of the inim-

itable [Dietrich]? *(Lester goes to the stereo and turns the record over.)*
OLLIE. You walk around like a pigeon. Why don't you light somewhere?
LESTER. Light?
OLLIE. I mean sit down somewhere since we've got to discuss the deal. We ain't discussed it yet.
LESTER. I discussed the deal with Cherry.
OLLIE. The deal has to be negotiated again, now that I've seen your elegant penthouse.
LESTER. Oh, but a deal is a deal. *(With a quick, agitated movement, Lester's hairpiece falls from his head to the floor.)*
OLLIE. Your hair come off.
LESTER. *(Picking up his toupee.)* I'm not bald.
OLLIE. Neither is a hen's egg.
LESTER. I had a little eczema on my scalp so I was advised to wear this hair piece till the condition cleared up. It will.
OLLIE. My price is a hundred, Les.
LESTER. Cherry said fifty.
OLLIE. Cherry hadn't seen your luxury penthouse, either, I reckon. Do you want me for my price? Or do I go?
LESTER. Cherry would be displeased. He doesn't like his boys to make separate deals.
OLLIE. Cherry's attitude don't always concern me much.
LESTER. I wouldn't dream of paying a hundred dollars to a —
OLLIE. Don't dream of it, just do it.
LESTER. — May I enquire what special endowments you have that are worth this exorbitant price?
OLLIE. I have the special endowment of a mutilation.
LESTER. — You have —
OLLIE. One arm. I have one arm, Les.
LESTER. — It's fortunate for you that I can afford to satisfy your demand.
OLLIE. Les, I have one arm.
LESTER. Dear boy, you said that before. I saw it. I didn't mention it, did I?
OLLIE. It don't hurt to repeat it.
LESTER. — I'm a lonely man.
OLLIE. I got one arm. I just have one arm, Les.
LESTER. Try to forget it, Ollie. I don't think about my hairpiece.
OLLIE. It took me a while to find out that johns like a mutilation,

as long as it's above the belt. One arm. I got one arm.
LESTER. You have — remarkable beauty.
OLLIE. When I walk down a street and look in a shop window, if I doubted the fact, the fact that I have one arm, it's visible to me! Not that I ever forget it! *(He has lost his cool.)* I'm sorry. Les, put the hundred where I can pick it up when I go, like on the mantel.
LESTER. You're not leaving before — ?
OLLIE. No. Not before. Not till after.
LESTER. *(Takes out his wallet and removes a hundred dollar bill.)* I can see that you wouldn't. Put it in your pocket now.
OLLIE. Thanks. *(Ollie begins to undress.)* You see I'm not leaving before. But time passes in this city faster than any I know. The clocks take Dexedrine and bennies. Speed!
LESTER. A wild idea occurred to me just now. Stay with me on a permanent basis. A while.
OLLIE. Les, I like you, but dismiss that idea.
LESTER. *(Sorrowfully.)* Impermanence is the order of civilization as I've observed it. Let me undress you, Ollie.
OLLIE. Even with one arm, I can dress and undress without assistance, Les.
LESTER. But to undress you would increase my pleasure. *(Lester undresses Ollie.)*
OLLIE. Les, I never let a man kiss me. I'm not gay trade.
LESTER. Oh, but —
OLLIE. No personal offense, Les.
LESTER. — May I touch your lips?
OLLIE. — Yes, Les. *(Lester places his finger on Ollie's lips.)*

Transition. A phone rings.

CHERRY. *(Picks up phone.)* Hey, It's Cherry. *(Beat.)* Well, you've certainly been laying low. I think I have just the right person for you. *(Beat.)* Yes, I'll send him over right away. *(He hangs up the phone.)* Ollie, I've got another friend that wants to meet you.
OLLIE. No, not now, Cherry.
CHERRY. It's gotta be now he's waitin' for you, he's ready —
OLLIE. Not now, Cherry, I need a break.

CHERRY. You need a break? When they're ready to pay, that means now.
OLLIE. Cherry, not now. I'm warning you.
CHERRY. You're warning me? If it wasn't for me you'd still be out on the street you cripple —
OLLIE. Who are you calling a cripple?! *(The other hustlers laugh. Ollie gives Cherry a series of slaps, each harder than the one before, and after each slap Cherry gasps. Ollie begins kicking him.)* Huh, Cherry?! Say it again, Cherry! Say it again!
CHERRY. You sonnovabitch!

Transition into jail.

NARRATOR/SEAN. Sedatives were put in his food the last few weeks, but the drugs were burned up in the furnace of his nerves. And the little sleep they gave him would plunge him into worse nightmares than the ones of waking. There was the prison chaplain …
CHAPLAIN. *(Reading tonelessly.)* "Yea, though I walk through the valley of the shadow of death, I will fear no evil, for thou art with me; thy rod and thy staff they comfort me — "
OLLIE. Shut up and get the hell away!
NARRATOR/SEAN. With the mechanical cruelty of the law, the execution of Oliver's sentence had given him several weeks in which to expect it and they were the weeks of summer. In his stifling cubicle there was very little to do while waiting for death and time enough with the impetus of disaster for the boy's malleable nature to be remolded still again.
OLLIE. *(He begins counting the letters.)* Seven hundred seventy-one. Seven hundred seventy-two. Seven hundred seventy-three. Seven hundred seventy-four. Seven hundred seventy-five …
NARRATOR/SEAN. The number? It was hard to tell, but during the last few weeks of his life, Ollie started counting every letter he received …
OLLIE. *(Continuing.)* Seven hundred seventy-six. Seven hundred seventy-seven. Seven hundred and —
GUARD. Four million six hundred and eighty-two, one million eight

hundred and two — *(He laughs.)* How many come for you, Ollie?

OLLIE. Don't interrupt me, I'm counting. *(The guard pushes a plate of food through a narrow opening in the bars and exits.)* Seven thousand eight hundred and ... *(Ollie holds his counting for a moment — he's lost his place — after a moment he figures it out and continues counting again ...)*

NARRATOR/SEAN. As the end of his little remaining period neared, he not only read them completely through but read them over again, and again.

OLLIE. *(He opens one particular letter and reads.)* Ollie. Know that I'm thinking of you in this difficult time. I've thought of you so often since that night we met. How vividly I remember your face. Us up on the terrace, overlooking Central Park. I hope everything will be cleared up soon. And when that happens you'll be free again. There was something about you, not only the physical thing, important as that was, which has made you haunt my mind since. *(Yelling to the guard.)* Hey! Hey!

GUARD. What?

OLLIE. Can I have me a pencil and paper?

GUARD. What are you gonna do? Write your mother?

OLLIE. What goddamn mother!

COMPANY MEMBER. Close up on Ollie.

NARRATOR/SEAN. Ollie began to answer some of the letters. Having no family or close friends to write to, this was his first attempt at writing letters and he wrote them, at first, with a laborious stiffness. The simplest sentence, at first, would knot up the muscles in his arm, and he found that printing was easier for him than ordinary writing. But as he went on — notice the stiffness going? — Soon the printed sentences gathered momentum just as springs clear out a channel for themselves after heavy rain. The sentences began to flow out of his less and less cramped fingers almost — Yes, expressively after a while, and to ring with the backwoods speech of the underprivileged South, to which had been added salty idioms of the underworld he had moved in, and the road and the sea.

OLLIE. Goddamn it —

NARRATOR/SEAN. He'd say, because he had to write with his left hand and he'd been right-handed. But into the letters went the warm and vivid talk that liquor and generous dealing had brought from his lips on certain occasions, the sort of talk that American tongues throw away so casually in bars and hotel bedrooms. The

cartoon symbol of laughter was often used, that heavily drawn —
OLLIE. "HA HA" —
NARRATOR/SEAN. *(Continuing.)* — with its tail of exclamatory punctuation — stars, spirals. And setting that down on paper, the
OLLIE. "HA HA" —
NARRATOR/SEAN. *(Continuing.)* — bit, was what gave him most relief.

Transition.

BARTENDER. What's your's, Ollie?
OLLIE. I'll have a — gimme a —
BARTENDER. What?
OLLIE. I reckon I'll have a bourbon and Coke. Gimme the bourbon fist and I'll put in the Coke if it's fizzing, I don't like a dead Coke. *(A man dressed for yachting emerges from one of the booths and approaches Ollie.)*
MAN. Young man, you have a wonderful voice. *(Beat.)* How'd you like to make two hundred dollars?
OLLIE. — Well, I'd be int'rested in knowing how to make it.
MAN. Something very simple.
OLLIE. Simple like what?
MAN. Appearing in a short movie I'm making on my yacht.
OLLIE. I'm not an actor.
MAN. Doesn't matter. All you have to do is — *(The man whispers something to Ollie.)*

Transition.

A "blue movie" is being made. Ollie, a woman, the yachtsman, and a few very wealthy guests are present. There are men behind a camera and equipment ready to shoot.

YACHTSMAN. Alright, quiet everybody. Camera's rolling … and … action. *(The woman strokes and kisses Ollie, moving up his leg. Ollie pulls away and stands up.)* Cut! It's not that difficult. She moves down your thigh, kisses your boot and then opens your belt. You get the idea?

OLLIE. Yeah, I get the idea, but do you? Can't you see I'm not fit for this?

YACHTSMAN. Baby you've got all the qualifications necessary. *(The camera crew and guests laugh at this.)* Try it again.

OLLIE. *(With fury.)* I get it. I understand it. The fact that I have one arm is the reason you wanted me for this freak show. You wanted a man that was mutilated! That was the qualification that you wanted. A beautiful girl doing things to a mutilated man, a man with one arm and the other a stump, a flipper. What you want is this girl's humiliation. You can shove it. I want out of this job. I want your launch to put me back on shore. Now! Meaning now!

YACHTSMAN. You don't have to do anything. She does it all. You just sit still and twist and moan a little. Can't you do that? Sit still and twist and moan like you were out of your skull? For two hundred dollars?

OLLIE. You didn' hear what I said? You thought I wasn't serious about it?

WOMAN. Please, baby.

YACHTSMAN. Yes baby, sit there. The camera is rolling. No sound this time. Lila, start with his fingers. And … action. Take her finger, wrap your lips around it, put it in your mouth … good … now kiss his right shoulder … a little further down … *(She reaches the stump.)* … kiss him there … lick him there … *(Ollie suddenly springs from the chair, kicks the camera over, and tears down lights.)*

OLLIE. Now is it still rolling, is it still rolling now?

YACHTSMAN. Young man, I think you oughta go up on deck and think it over. *(Ollie exits. Then the yachtsman speaks to the girl.)* Lila, go up on deck with him. Explain how simple it is. *(Then to a film crew member.)* You! Fix that light! *(The woman follows after Ollie. Ollie, at the rail, is looking out at the sea. The woman enters.)*

WOMAN. Honey, you shouldn't have done that. It could have cost us two hundred dollars each.

OLLIE. When he told you to —

WOMAN. I know, but, honey, it didn't matter to me.

OLLIE. I used to respect myself. Didn't you? Didn't you, ever?
WOMAN. Never much.
OLLIE. I respected myself until I lost one arm.
WOMAN. Let's not talk about self-respect, or losing it, or how.
OLLIE. It's important to have it and a sick thing to lose it.
WOMAN. Would it make it easier for you if we — *(She moves in to kiss him, he won't allow it.)*
OLLIE. They want to humiliate me.
WOMAN. I don't think of it that way.
OLLIE. Then what way do you think of it?
WOMAN. A way to make two hundred dollars.
OLLIE. Even with one arm I could drive this launch back to shore. Let's get the hell off this yacht, and out of this dirty business.
WOMAN. Ollie? I need the two hundred dollars.
OLLIE. I'm scared to stay here.
WOMAN. Scared of what?
OLLIE. I'm scared that I might kill him. I could with just one arm and I might do it.
WOMAN. You know what you ought to do, baby? Don't think of it as anything but a job, a night job that you can forget in the morning.
OLLIE. Can't we still have a little self-respect? Just a little? *(She slips her hand inside his robe.)*
WOMAN. Self-respect can be put away for a while.
OLLIE. I never thought the lights on a shore could semaphore to you: "Come back, hurry, quick, before you … "
WOMAN. Ollie, go through it for me and then we'll go back to the shore.
OLLIE. You don't feel disgust?
WOMAN. With you, no, I feel pleasure, which is a rare thing for me.
OLLIE. I hate hearing him tell you to do unnatural things to me like he tells you in his oily voice with his fat wet-mouth grin.
WOMAN. Two hundred dollars is two hundred dollars and I need it bad.
OLLIE. What are we?
WOMAN. — Don't think about it. It's me that does it to you. I like doing it, so you don't have to think. Come on. Please. For me. Let's get it over with. Quick! *(Ollie gives in. They begin to shoot again.)*

Transition to Ollie and the Yachtsman alone. They have finished filming.

YACHTSMAN. Job well done. The launch will come back for you later. You have the privilege of getting to know me better.
OLLIE. I think I could live without that. When do I get paid?
YACHTSMAN. Don't sweat it, baby. What's your drink? *(As the Yachtsman begins to touch Ollie, he becomes enraged and, grabbing a metal bookend, beats the Yachtsman.)* Stop, Ollie. Stop! Stop! *(Ollie kills the Yachtsman.)*

Transition.

The interior of the yacht transforms back into prison.

NARRATOR/SEAN. Everything went against him at the short trial. Did he want it that way? The defense of Ollie was particularly hopeless when he admitted that he had removed from the dead man's body a wallet containing several hundred dollars. These things assured the conviction of Ollie and doomed him to the electric chair.

Transition.

Ollie is sitting on his cot, disheveled, rocking.

OLLIE. *(Mumbling at first, then screaming to the guard in crescendo.)* Is it day or night? Night or day? *(The guard slips his food into his cell.)* Is it day or night?
GUARD. It's February fourteenth — Valentine's Day.
OLLIE. *(Exhausted, panting for breath.)* Day or night. I got no way

to know, no window to look through, have I? With this electric light that hangs over me all the time. Can't it be turned off?
GUARD. I put your supper through the slot.
OLLIE. A paper plate of slop with a paper spoon. *(Ollie kicks the food out of his cell.)*
GUARD. You tryin' to starve yourself to death before you go to the chair?
OLLIE. What do I need with food?
GUARD. If you go on not eatin' you're gonna git fed through a pipe in a vein.
OLLIE. Why can't you turn that big, enormous light off when it's night so I can sleep?
GUARD. You're in the birdcage now, and it's always lighted.
OLLIE. Can't I have something to tie around my eyes?
GUARD. It's night. When I say here's your breakfast, you'll know its morning, when I say here's your supper you'll know its night.
OLLIE. Jesus, Jesus, not human.
GUARD. Ollie, you got to live with it, till you die.
OLLIE. Turn off the light, you bastards! Turn off the light! Nobody can live day and night under a light like a sun that don't set! Cut off the light! Cut it off!
NARRATOR/SEAN. The city that had appointed his death could not be oblivious to Ollie, and so the next day his picture, the picture of a legend, appeared again in a newspaper. A copy of the paper was delivered to the home of a divinity student. Ollie's face looked at him. The caption read:
DIVINITY STUDENT. "Condemned Youth Refuses Consolation of Faith." *(The divinity student walks around the room, disturbed, always returning to take another glance at Ollie's haunting photograph.)*
NARRATOR/SEAN. The article spoke of the hard and unrepentant nature of the boy who was to die very soon and of his violent behavior in the prison. But the picture of Ollie was incongruous to those facts. The student thought that the face of the blond youth had a tender beauty, of the sort that some painter of the Renaissance might have slyly attributed to a juvenile saint. Was it the article or the face that disturbed the student so much? It was probably both. Thinking about the boy so obsessed the young minister that he would pace about his living room as if it were Ollie's cell, and he kept returning to the picture of Ollie's face in the paper.

GUARD. He doesn't want a chaplain.
DIVINITY STUDENT. Sir, I'm not a chaplain.
GUARD. What are you?
DIVINITY STUDENT. I'm a seminary student.
GUARD. The execution is tomorrow, don't you rattle him.
DIVINITY STUDENT. No, I won't sir.
GUARD. Suit yourself.

Transition.

The guard opens the cell door for the divinity student.

GUARD. Visitor for you. *(Ollie is seated only in a pair of shorts on the edge of his cot. The divinity student enters and the guard returns to his post. The student immediately removes a small paper box from a pocket, takes out several little white tablets, and stuffs them in his mouth.)*
DIVINITY STUDENT. I have come to see you.
OLLIE. I reckon you have. What did you take out of that box?
DIVINITY STUDENT. Pills for a — condition.
OLLIE. What's the condition?
DIVINITY STUDENT. A little on-again-off-again functional disturbance of the heart. In this condition my mouth turns very dry. Could I have some water? *(Ollie fills an enameled tin cup at a tap in a corner of the cell.)* Thank you.
OLLIE. You don't have to whisper. The guard is at the end of the corridor. What have you come here for?
DIVINITY STUDENT. *(Still whispering.)* Why, uh — just for a talk.
OLLIE. I got nothing to say except — tomorrow I go.
DIVINITY STUDENT. Go where.
OLLIE. To the chair.
DIVINITY STUDENT. — Oh. It takes a minute or two for the,

uh, condition to, uh, subside. Is there — can I — a place to sit down —

OLLIE. Sit on that stool there.

DIVINITY STUDENT. Oh. Yes. Thank you. May I — I'd like to — read you something.

OLLIE. What?

DIVINITY STUDENT. The twenty-first Psalm.

OLLIE. I tole 'em I didn't want no chaplain in here.

DIVINITY STUDENT. Oh, I'm not a chaplain, I'm a seminary student. And also a stranger to you with sympathy for the misunderstood in the world.

OLLIE. Then you got sympathy for a good many people. Huh?

DIVINITY STUDENT. Yes, I have, I'm afraid so … Are you prepared for tomorrow?

OLLIE. I'm not prepared for the hot seat but the seat is prepared for me.

DIVINITY STUDENT. I'm talking about eternity that waits for us all.

OLLIE. It can afford to wait as long as it wants to. Eternity. A man can't wait that long. Can he? No, he can't. Especially when he's got a date with the chair tomorrow. Not day after tomorrow but early tomorrow. Look. I got a cellmate.

DIVINITY STUDENT. — Do you mean me?

OLLIE. I was talkin' about that fly that's buzzin' around in here. He's got more eternity going for him than I have going for me. Ha?

DIVINITY STUDENT. Would you like me to try to swat it with one of these magazines?

OLLIE. No. A fly as a cellmate is better than nothing at all. I'll tell you something. I've been lonely in here, and the loneliness don't get lesser, it gets bigger. Now it's the size of a mountain and it's built on me.

DIVINITY STUDENT. Would you let me give you a cross to carry with you? *(Pause.)*

OLLIE. That's a nice offer but the prison chaplain will have a cross.

DIVINITY STUDENT. Please take it from me. I want to give it to you. Afterwards it would be returned to me. That is, if I ask for it. Look at it. *(A gold cross with an amethyst in the center.)*

OLLIE. I would take it if I was able to hock it, but the offer was nice.

DIVINITY STUDENT. This world of ours —

OLLIE. It's no world of mine.

DIVINITY STUDENT. — This world of ours, yours, mine, everybody's – this transitory existence is just a threshold, a stepping stone to something immense beyond.

OLLIE. Yes. Death is immense but there's no stepping stone to nothing but an unvarnished pine box.

DIVINITY STUDENT. Try to meet your Savior in a state of grace — You are face to face with the last and greatest adventure —

OLLIE. Bull.

DIVINITY STUDENT. I wish that you would believe me.

OLLIE. I was a boxer. A good one. *(Then with the sad, quiet pride that always accompanies this statement, he continues.)* I was light heavyweight champion of the Pacific Fleet. Then I lost one arm. Can you explain that to me?

DIVINITY STUDENT. It could be that you were in error.

OLLIE. No, that's what I was — till I lost one arm.

DIVINITY STUDENT. I think that you were in error and didn't know it and persisted in error.

OLLIE. I wasn't driving the car. I yelled at the kid that was drivin', "Slow down, you fucker." We entered an underpass. The underpass of my life. The kid that was drivin' was drunk. Not competent to drive. Then came, in the underpass of our lives, the crash. They never came true. I mean to. Skulls busted wide open. Like a bean is busted open when you're shellin' beans. I was what they call the survivor. What sort of survival? A boxer with one arm torn off him. All right. I mean all wrong. Can you explain that to me?

DIVINITY STUDENT. It — It —

OLLIE. — It — It?

DIVINITY STUDENT. It gave you the chance of a lifetime.

OLLIE. Chance for what? Being reduced to a hustler?

DIVINITY STUDENT. A chance to grow your spiritual arms and reach for God.

OLLIE. I don't reach for nobody till they reach for me. *(The student puts hand on Ollie.)*

DIVINITY STUDENT. Don't think of me as a man but as a connection.

OLLIE. Shit! A connection is a man pushing dope.

DIVINITY STUDENT. I am —

OLLIE. You are what? What are you? Now, I'm whispering like you. Is this conversation a secret?

DIVINITY STUDENT. It's a private communion between you

and me. What I am, what you must let me be, is a wire plugged in your heart and charged with God's message to you. *(Pause. Ollie stares at his visitor.)* I see that you've received a great many letters.

OLLIE. I been all over this country and gotten to know many people. I've forgotten most of 'em but they've remembered me. For a long while here I paid no attention to the letters. Now I answer them. I try to remember each one of these men, and if I had a little more time before tomorrow, yes, I think it's tomorrow, they don't give me the time here, I think I'd answer them all. *(He grabs one of his letters.)* Would you like to hear it and see if the grammar's okay? — I'll read it to you out loud. *(He reads the letter.)* "Yes, I remember you plainly. I met you in the park in back of the public library or was it in the men's room of the Greyhound depot? I met so many, sometimes I get them mixed up a little. However, you stand out plainly. You said to me, son, can you direct me to the art museum and then we got to talking and the first thing I knew we was in your duplex apartment on the lakefront and you offered me a drink. I asked for my favorite drink, which is Five-Star Hennessy and you had some. And how is the Windy City of Chicago now that it's summer again? I sure would appreciate feeling those cool lake breezes and pouring down a few shots of that Five-Star Hennessy where we shacked up that day. I tell you it's hot in this cooler and it's going to get hotter before it gets cooler again. *(To the Divinity Student.)* Do you know what I mean? *(Divinity Student nods. Then back to letter.)* I guess you would like to know if I'm afraid. The answer is yes. I don't look forward to it a bit in the world. After I lost my arm I seemed to go through a change which I can't account for except I stopped caring what happened to me. That is to say I lost my self-respect. I went all over the country without any plans except to keep on moving. I picked up strangers in every city I went to. I had experiences with them that only meant money to me and a place to shack up for the night-liquor, liquor-food. I never thought it could mean very much to them. Now all these letters like yours have proved it did. I meant to them something important, yes, to hundreds of people whose faces and names had slipped clean out of my mind almost as soon as I left them. — Now I feel like I have run up a debt of some kind to all these people. Not money but feelings. I would leave them sometimes without even saying goodbye. I can't imagine how these men could forgive me. If I had known then, I mean when I was outside,

I guess I would have felt there was more to live for. Anyhow now the situation is hopeless. All will be over for me in a very short while. Ha ha! Tomorrow? *(Pause.)* Letters. Words. How long will they remember Ollie Olsen?

DIVINITY STUDENT. — I doubt that — don't think that — they will ever forget you.

OLLIE. Wet that towel for me, will you?

DIVINITY STUDENT. It's not a very clean towel.

OLLIE. Clean enough.

DIVINITY STUDENT. What do you want to do with this towel?

OLLIE. I don't want to do nothing with it. I want you to do something with it. *(Ollie removes his shirt.)*

DIVINITY STUDENT. What?

OLLIE. Wipe the sweat off my back.

DIVINITY STUDENT. I — I — *(The divinity student doesn't move.)*

OLLIE. Do I smell bad to you or something.

DIVINITY STUDENT. No. — No.

OLLIE. I am clean. I was given a shower.

DIVINITY STUDENT. Yes. Yes. *(The student begins rubbing his back.)*

OLLIE. I have always been careful to keep myself clean. I was a very clean fighter — and a very clean whore — did you know that I was a whore?

DIVINITY STUDENT. — No.

OLLIE. Well, that's what I was all right, and all those letters are from people that had me as a whore on the street. After boxing was finished by having one arm, my second profession was whoring. *(The student approaches him as if he was a dangerous animal and begins to rub Ollie's back.)* Go on. Why'd you stop?

DIVINITY STUDENT. I — I —

OLLIE. If you don't like the towel, you can rub with your hands. *(He arches his body a little and pulls his shorts further down his back.)* Go on. Rub with your hands. They're cleaner than the towel.

DIVINITY STUDENT. No, no, please, I can't, no!

OLLIE. Don't be a fool. There's a door at the end of the hall. It makes a noise if anybody comes in it.

DIVINITY STUDENT. I'll go, now. Yes, I'll go now. *(Quick as a panther, Ollie springs up and catches his wrist.)*

OLLIE. Wait! You've seen the pile of letters sent to me. They're bills from people I owe. Not money but feelings. For three whole

years I went all over the country stirring up feelings without feeling nothin' myself. Now that's all changed and I have feelings myself: I'm lonely and bottled up the same as you are. Oh, I know you, your type. Everything is artistic or else it's religious or talk too educated for Ollie Olsen. Come off it. All that stuff's a mountain of bullshit. I don't buy it. I'm clean. And you? Aren't you clean? Take me so I can pay back. Hell, man, little man, all you need like 'em all needed, if they needed, is less than a push on the head …
DIVINITY STUDENT. Guard! Guard! God! *(The guard comes running to let the divinity student out of the cell. He has to be lifted and half carried down the corridor. They exit. Ollie is left alone.)*
OLLIE. Maybe he'll come back tonight. *(Transition. Light change/shift. Sound effects. The guards and the warden and the chaplain are in Ollie's cell.)* I wanna take 'em with me.
WARDEN. A few of the letters?
OLLIE. All of 'em. I want 'em with me.
WARDEN. In the room?
OLLIE. Some of 'em in the chair with me.
WARDEN. Son, they'd burn.
OLLIE. That's all right. Me and the letters together.
WARDEN. Son, I can't.
OLLIE. It's a request, the last one.
WARDEN. The newspaper people will wonder what they're —
OLLIE. Let 'em wonder. I want all my letters with me.
WARDEN. Where do you want them, Ollie?
OLLIE. Some of 'em in the chair with me and the rest where I can see 'em.
CHAPLAIN. It would distract him from prayer.
OLLIE. I'm not gonna pray or listen to you praying.
WARDEN. I'll have them carried in.
OLLIE. Let me carry some.
WARDEN. Which ones?
OLLIE. Any. These. *(The warden nods.)* Thanks. *(Light change/shift. Sound effects. There is a processional of Ollie to the chair. The chaplain recites a prayer throughout. They bring him to the chair and ritualistically prepare him with the shackles. The Chaplain recites the Lord's Prayer.)*
GUARD. Oliver Olsen, you've been condemned to die by a jury of your peers. Sentencing imposed by a judge in good standing in this state. Electricity shall now be passed through your body until

you are dead in accordance with state law. God have mercy on your soul.

NARRATOR/SEAN. Then the moment came. Then a bolt from across the frontiers of the unknown was channeled through Ollie's body for one instant, and a second, and a third … and then swept back having claimed the boy whose lost right arm had been known as "lightning in leather." *(Light change/shift. Sound effects. The letters remain in the chair.)* The body, unclaimed after death, had been turned over to a medical college to be used in a classroom laboratory. The students who performed the dissection were somewhat abashed by the body under their knives. It seemed intended for some more august purpose, to stand in a gallery of antique sculpture, touched only by light through stillness and contemplation, for it had the nobility of some broken Apollo that no one was likely to carve so purely again. But death has never been much in the way of completion. *(Lights.)*

End of Play

PROPERTY LIST

Letters
Trash can
Tamales
Keys
Hot dog
Handkerchief
Umbrella
Matches
Towel
Blond toupee
Food tray
Newspaper
Small paper box with white tablets inside
Enameled tin cup
Magazines
Gold cross with amethyst center
Dirty towel

SOUND EFFECTS

Seagull
Boxing bell
Cars zooming by
Car crash
Piano (blues)
Phone